LEADERS AND MANAGERS

HOW WE NEED BOTH TO BUILD AND HAVE A SUCCESSFUL COMPANY OR ORGANIZATION

BY DOVE NIGHT MPA

In every organization or company, there always a person who is responsible for the control and detail in the company .This is the person who gives his employees the tasks, and he checks to see if they are doing what they supposed to do. He hires or fires the c players, and he rewards the A players (or the best) in his or her organization. This person is the manager. How this person works is critical to the success of the company. Then there is the person who is the innovator, the person who has a vision and wants to make big changes for the company. This person is usually the CEO, or the department head, which comes up with big ideas, and works with groups, inside and outside the organization to make dreams happen. When this person makes a decision, he can change how the program works or how the entire organization operates. This person is important to the business of an organization. Let's s learn more about how

managers work within an organization.

Leadership v. Management?
Leadership or Management

1. Managers administer; Leaders innovate.
2. Managers ask how and when; Leaders ask what and why.
3. Managers focus on systems; Leaders focus on people.
4. Managers do things right; Leaders do the right things.
5. Managers maintain; Leaders develop.
6. Managers rely on control; Leaders inspire trust.
7. Managers have short-term perspective; Leaders have long-term perspective.
8. Managers accept the status-quo; Leaders challenge the status-quo.
9. Managers have an eye on the bottom line; Leaders have an eye on the horizon.
10. Managers imitate; Leaders originate.
11. Managers emulate the classic good soldier; Leaders are their own person.
12. Managers copy; Leaders show originality.

Source: http://thecolostepperbentierblogspot.com/2010/11/leadership-vs-management.html

LEADING

- Vision & strategy
- Creating value
- Influence & inspiration
- Have followers
- Leading people
- People focused
- Charismatic style
- Risk & change seekers
- Appeal to the heart
- Proactive
- Sets direction
- Raising expectations
- Ask questions

Overlap

- Accomplish a goal
- Explain vision
- Organization figureheads
- Motivate others
- Mobilize resources

MANAGING

- Policies & procedures
- Counting value
- Power & control
- Have subordinates
- Managing work
- Work focused
- Authoritarian style
- Risk averse & stability
- Appeal to the head
- Reactive
- Plans detail
- Maintain status quo
- Give directions

Leader	Manager
Copes with change	Copes with complexity
Challenges the status quo	Works with the status quo
Asks Why	Asks What
Plans long term	Plans short term
Aligns people	Organizes people
Motivates and inspires	Administrates and control
Focuses of people	Focuses on systems and structures
Communicates and delivers the Vision	Follows the vision
Looks into the future	Works in the present

manager	leader
Oversees the current process well	Wants to create the future
Must achieve balance	Needs to make change
Thinks execution	Thinks ideas
Comfortable with control	Welcomes risks
Problems are just that, and need resolution ASAP	Sees problems as opportunities, is patient
Procedure is King	Substance trumps the King
Instructs as to technique and process	Your best college Professor
Impersonal, remote	High Emotional Intelligence

MANAGERS

While both leaders and managers deal with power, and influence. Managers in a company deals with responsibility and accountability to an organization.

Management is usually formal authority that is given to a person from a higher authority. They usually are involved in transactional activities such as setting work assignments, they are task oriented and gives rewards to their employees such as giving raises for exemplary work or give punishments such as fire or lay off employees who are not following the rules or who are not doing good work. Managers usually value order, rules and control. Managers keep the organization running smoothly, creating the stability that is needed to keep the organization healthy and in flux.

MANAGER	LEADER
- Planning and budgeting	- Charts a course providing direction
- Organizing and staffing	- Provides guidance and counsel
- Follows orders	- People follow their example
- Controlling and solves problems	- Motivates and inspires
- Maintains control and order	- Creates an environment for change
- Protects status quo	- Builds relationships and trust
- Writes memorandums	- Trains and teaches
- Follows rules and regulations	- Questions rules and regulations
- Technical orientation	- Strategic orientation

MANAGERS:
(who are not leaders)
- Relate Position to Position
- Rely on their authority
- Have compliant subordinates
- Use command and control tactics
- Follow prescribed procedures, rules, policies and regulations
- Are given the manager role
- Play it safe

LEADERS:
- Relate Person to Person
- Use influence beyond authority
- Have committed followers
- Use interpersonal influence
- Do more than what is prescribed and employ creativity and innovation
- Take the leadership role
- Are willing to take responsible risks

Leadership vs. Management

Understanding the difference is the first step to understanding one's role as a leader.

Leaders lead people	Managers manage things
Leaders are needed in times of change	Managers are needed to improve and keep the status quo

pg. 19

LEADERS

Leaders gain power from no higher authority. Leaders are inspirational, charismatic, and visionary. They are usually involved in transformational activities with their employees by empowering them, coaching them by letting them make choices instead of forcing it upon them. They are always involved in creating changes that can alter the entire organization. Leaders can break the rules and change an organization for the better.

Leaders are usually charismatic, have very big goals. They drive the entire organization through a vision. They have a vision that is implemented by the organization; it's for employees to follow.

Some examples of great leaders are Franklin D Roosevelt, Abraham Lincoln, Martin Luther King Jr and Bill Gates.

Leaders are inspirational and they inspire their employees

or peers through choice and change.

Leaders inspire people to want to do something. **Managers** hold people **accountable** for doing something.

sentis — sentis.net

The organization's administration is both leaders and managers

Every CEO, president, director, administrator, vice president or manager of a company or organization were both leaders and managers .They each sometimes run the place by making sure the organization is running smoothly and sometimes they try to create new changes by working on a mission, or vision that will lead their organization to success by the accomplishment of a long term goal that permanently changes the organization for the better, sooner or later.

EXAMPLE OF LEADERSHIP AND GONE WRONG! In 1789 KING LOUIS XVI was the leader of his country yet his indecisiveness, and lack of cohesive leadership experience and inspiration had driven his country citizens into revolt. It was because the economy in France in the eighteenth century went downhill due to inflation, and the high taxes put on the peasants by the monarchy while the very privileged paid very little in tax. This lead to his death by the guillotine during the French revolution in 1793.

Example of leadership and management gone right!

Take a look at Abraham Lincoln and how he led North America through the civil war; Take a look at England's

Queen Elizabeth I and how she led her country in the war with Spain in 1558. Martin Luther King Jr's inspiration in leading his followers to overcome segregation in the 1950s and 60s.

Other leaders can include, Bill Gates, Oprah winfrey, Barack Obama and his leadership in capturing Osama bin laden in 2011. Anybody can be an effective leader or manager, it just takes guts and the ability to learn from one's experiences.

www.ingramcontent.com/pod-product-compliance
Lightning Source LLC
Chambersburg PA
CBHW041117180526
45172CB00001B/285